Classic
THAI

Classic
THAI

Subtle and aromatic recipes from the East

KIT CHAN

SMITHMARK

This edition published in 1997 by
SMITHMARK Publishers, a division of US Media Holdings, Inc.
16 East 32nd Street
New York, New York 10016

SMITHMARK books are available for bulk purchase for sales promotion and for premium use. For details write or call
the manager of special sales, SMITHMARK Publishers, 16 East 32nd Street, New York, New York 10016; (212) 532-6600.

Produced by Anness Publishing Limited
Hermes House
88-89 Blackfriars Road
London SE1 8HA

ISBN 0 7651 9571 2

Publisher: Joanna Lorenz
Senior Food Editor: Linda Fraser
Project Editor: Zoe Antoniou
Designer: Annie Moss
Mac Artist: John Fowler
Illustrator: Madeleine David
Jacket Photographer: Thomas Odulate
Food Stylist: Kit Chan

Printed and bound in Singapore

Picture on frontispiece: Steamed Seafood Packets, Spring Rolls, Pork Satay and Golden Pouches

1 3 5 7 9 10 8 6 4 2

Contents

Introduction

Thailand is probably one of the most diverse and complex countries in Asia. Geographically, it is halfway between India and China, and the rich cultures of these next-door neighbors have influenced the development of its national cuisine.

Thailand is divided into five regions that have distinct geographical and cultural differences ranging from dense jungles and mountainous retreats to vast rice paddies, untamed rivers, sandy beaches and the warm, clear ocean.

The climate is tropical, so there is an abundance of fruit, vegetables and flowers. Indeed, freshly picked vegetables, aromatic herbs and flavorful leaves are essential to Thai cooking. Vegetables may be stir-fried, steamed or boiled.

The carving of fruits and vegetables into exotic sculptures, decorated with flowers and foliage, has become an art form in Thailand. Thailand also boasts over one thousand varieties of orchids, and the orchid has become an emblem for the country.

In Thailand, food is a celebration. To have to eat alone ranks high on the scale of misfortunes. Throughout Thailand, food and snacking are essential aspects of life, and there is a constant supply of spicy tidbits available everywhere.

The variety of snacks is huge. Some dishes are small, such as savory pastries, spring rolls, steamed dumplings and rice balls. Others, such as noodle dishes, are more substantial and can be a meal in themselves. These snacks are not considered real food in Asia, but merely a pleasurable diversion, a nibble between meals or a treat at the market. Appetizers as such are not common in Thai meals because generally all the dishes are brought to the table at once.

Cooking in Thailand is a source of pride and wonder. A Thai cook will always strive for a balance of flavor, texture and color in a dish. Presentation varies from simple plastic bowls at sidewalk stands to beautifully decorated china and artistic displays in the finer restaurants, but the complexity of taste and flavor is consistent.

A Thai meal offers a combination of flavors: sweet, hot, sour, salty and sometimes bitter. Thailand offers a tropical cornucopia of good things to eat, and the coastal region yields an abundance of seafood, both tempting and exotic. Usually, in addition to the obligatory bowl of rice, a variety of dishes will be offered, including a soup, a curry, a steamed dish, a fried one, a salad and one or two sauces.

Opposite (clockwise from top): three classic rice and noodle dishes; Fried Jasmine Rice, Pad Thai and Special Chow Mein.

Above (clockwise from top): lemongrass, Thai shallots, kaffir limes and fresh kaffir lime leaves.

There should be no duplication or repetition, and ingredients and colors should be as diverse as possible. This reflects the influence of the Chinese principle of yin and yang; the idea is to achieve overall healthful harmony by balancing opposing qualities. The portion size will depend on the number of people eating. All the dishes are placed on the table at the same time and shared. They are not eaten in any particular order.

Water and tea are the most common drinks served with a meal. Thai whiskey is often drunk at festive gatherings. But soup is also a very significant part of daily fare in Thailand. It can be served as a snack or a light lunch. A bowl of soup is nearly always included in a Thai meal. It is placed on the table alongside the other dishes, to be enjoyed as a liquid refreshment as and when each diner chooses.

Equipment (right, clockwise from top): two-tier bamboo steamer, large granite mortar and pestle, wooden cutting board with cleaver, large cook's knife and small paring knife, wire-basket, draining spoon and wok.

Thai soups, which are quick and easy to prepare, are usually based on a light broth, and many, such as Pumpkin and Coconut Soup, are enriched with coconut milk or cream.

Without a doubt the most famous soup is *Tom Yam Goong* – Hot and Sour Shrimp Soup with Lemongrass – a symphony of flavors that uses many local favorites such as lemongrass,

Chilies, clockwise from top: green, Thai orange, Indian, red and mild green.

galangal, cilantro, kaffir lime leaves and chilies.

Indeed, the most prevalent flavor in Thai cooking comes from the chili which, surprisingly, was introduced to the country during the sixteenth century by Portuguese missionaries. It didn't take Thai cooks long to make good use of it, and they came to believe that chilies cool the body, stimulate the appetite and bring balance and harmony to food.

Curries are also a prominent part of a selection of dishes in a main meal. All curry-making begins with the curry paste. Years ago, each household would have its own recipes, handed down from generation to generation. To make the pastes, various herbs and spices are crushed with a mortar and pestle, resulting in an aromatic and fragrant wet paste that can range from mild to extremely hot. The hottest are the green curry pastes.

Curries originated in southern India, but unlike Indian curries that use a lot of dried powdered spices and are thick and simmer for many hours, Thai curries are fresher and much lighter. They are usually thin and soup-like and require a lot less cooking, with the exception of the dish known as Mussaman curry.

In earlier times, Thais were accustomed to eating with their fingers, pressing rice into small balls that were dipped into other dishes. Today, they eat with a large spoon to scoop up sauces, and a fork to mix and push food onto the spoon. Knives are rarely used because meat is usually served in very small pieces and chopsticks are used only to eat Chinese-style noodles.

Thais tend to cook by "feel," taking into account the tastes and preferences of their family. You should always taste and adjust the seasoning as you are cooking. In particular, if you are not used to the hotness of chilies, add a little at a time until you achieve the desired balance. In short, Thai cuisine is light and fresh, with delicately balanced spices and a harmony of flavors, colors and textures designed to appeal to both the eyes and the palate. It may take some time for a novice to grasp the idea of preparing so many dishes, but the rewards are great for there is something here for everyone.

STEAMED SEAFOOD PACKETS

These neat and delicate steamed packets make an excellent appetizer or a light lunch. You can find banana leaves in Asian or Caribbean markets.

INGREDIENTS
8 ounces crabmeat
2 ounces shelled shrimp, chopped
6 water chestnuts, chopped
2 tablespoons chopped bamboo shoots
1 tablespoon chopped scallion
1 teaspoon chopped ginger
1 tablespoon soy sauce
1 tablespoon Thai fish sauce
12 rice paper sheets
banana leaves
oil, for brushing
2 scallions, shredded
2 red chilies, seeded and sliced,
and cilantro leaves, to garnish

SERVES 4

1 Combine the crabmeat, chopped shrimp, water chestnuts, bamboo shoots, chopped scallion and ginger in a bowl. Mix well, then add the soy sauce and fish sauce. Stir until blended.

2 Take a sheet of rice paper and dip it in warm water. Place it on a flat surface and let soften for a few seconds.

3 Place a spoonful of the filling in the center of the sheet and fold into a square packet. Repeat with the rest of the rice paper and seafood mixture.

4 Use banana leaves to line a steamer, then brush them with oil. Place the packets, seam-side down, on the leaves and steam over high heat for 6–8 minutes or until the filling is cooked.

5 Transfer to a plate and serve, garnished with the shredded scallions, sliced chilies and cilantro.

COOK'S TIP
The seafood packets will spread out when steamed, so be sure to allow plenty of space between them to prevent them from sticking together.

GOLDEN POUCHES

hese crisp pouches are delicious served as an appetizer or to accompany drinks at a party.

INGREDIENTS
4 ounces ground pork
4 ounces crabmeat
2–3 wood ears, soaked and chopped
1 tablespoon chopped cilantro
1 teaspoon chopped garlic
2 tablespoons chopped scallions
1 egg
1 tablespoon Thai fish sauce
1 teaspoon soy sauce
pinch of sugar
20 wonton wrappers
20 long chives, blanched (optional)
oil, for deep frying
freshly ground black pepper
plum or sweet chili sauce, to serve

MAKES ABOUT 20

1 In a mixing bowl, combine the pork, crabmeat, wood ears, cilantro, garlic, scallions and egg. Mix well and season with fish sauce, soy sauce, sugar and freshly ground black pepper.

2 Take a wonton wrapper and place it on a flat surface. Put a heaping teaspoon of filling in the center of the wrapper, then pull the edges of the wrapper around the filling.

3 Pinch together to seal. If desired, you can go a step further and tie the packet with a long chive. Repeat with the remaining pork mixture and wonton wrappers.

4 Heat the oil in a wok or deep-fat fryer. Fry the wontons in batches until they are crisp and golden brown. Drain on paper towels and serve immediately with either plum or sweet chili sauce.

PORK SATAY

Satay, which originated in Indonesia, are skewers of meat marinated with spices and grilled quickly over charcoal. You can also make them with chicken, beef or lamb.

INGREDIENTS
1 pound pork tenderloin
1 teaspoon grated ginger
1 lemongrass stalk, finely chopped
3 garlic cloves, finely chopped
1 tablespoon medium curry paste
1 teaspoon ground cumin
1 teaspoon ground turmeric
¼ cup coconut cream
2 tablespoons Thai fish sauce
1 teaspoon granulated sugar
20 wooden satay skewers
oil, for brushing
mint sprigs, to garnish

FOR THE SATAY SAUCE
1 cup coconut milk
2 tablespoons red curry paste
½ cup crunchy peanut butter
½ cup chicken stock
3 tablespoons brown sugar
2 tablespoons tamarind juice
1 tablespoon Thai fish sauce
½ teaspoon salt

MAKES ABOUT 20

1 Cut the pork thinly into 2-inch strips. Combine the ginger, lemongrass, garlic, medium curry paste, cumin, turmeric, coconut cream, fish sauce and sugar.

2 Pour the mixture over the pork and allow to marinate for about 2 hours.

3 Meanwhile, make the sauce. Heat the coconut milk over medium heat, then add the red curry paste, peanut butter, chicken stock and sugar.

4 Cook and stir until smooth, for 5–6 minutes. Add the tamarind juice, fish sauce and salt to taste.

5 Thread the meat onto skewers. Brush with oil and grill over charcoal or under the broiler for 3–4 minutes on each side, turning occasionally, until cooked. Garnish with mint and serve with the satay sauce.

SPRING ROLLS

These crunchy spring rolls are as popular in Thai cuisine as they are in Chinese. Thais use garlic, pork and noodles as a filling. Serve the rolls with Thai sweet chili sauce for dipping, if desired.

INGREDIENTS
4–6 dried Chinese mushrooms, soaked
2 ounces bean thread noodles, soaked
vegetable oil, for frying
2 garlic cloves, chopped
2 red chilies, seeded and chopped
8 ounces ground pork
2 ounces chopped cooked shrimp
2 tablespoons Thai fish sauce
1 teaspoon granulated sugar
1 carrot, finely chopped
2 ounces bamboo shoots, chopped
2 ounces bean sprouts
2 scallions, chopped
1 tablespoon chopped cilantro
2 tablespoons flour
twenty-four 6-inch square
spring roll wrappers
freshly ground black pepper

MAKES ABOUT 24

1 Drain and chop the mushrooms. Drain the noodles and cut into 2-inch lengths.

2 Heat 2 tablespoons of oil in a wok or frying pan, add the garlic and chilies, and fry for 30 seconds. Add the pork and stir until the meat is browned.

3 Add the noodles, mushrooms and shrimp. Season with fish sauce, sugar and pepper. Transfer to a bowl.

4 Mix in the carrot, bamboo shoots, bean sprouts, scallions and chopped cilantro for the filling. Reserve a little of the mixture to use as a garnish.

5 In a bowl, mix the flour to a paste with a little water. Place a spoonful of filling in the center of a spring roll wrapper.

6 Turn the bottom edge over to cover the filling, then fold in the left and right sides. Roll up almost to the top edge. Brush the top edge with flour paste and seal. Repeat with the rest of the wrappers.

7 Heat some oil in a wok or deep-fat fryer. Slide in the spring rolls a few at a time and fry until crisp and golden brown. Remove with a slotted spoon and drain on paper towels. Serve hot, garnished with the reserved vegetables.

PAN-STEAMED MUSSELS WITH THAI HERBS

nother simple dish to prepare. The lemongrass adds a refreshing tang to the mussels.

INGREDIENTS

2–3 pounds mussels, cleaned and
beards removed
2 lemongrass stalks, finely chopped
4 shallots, chopped
4 kaffir lime leaves, roughly torn
2 red chilies, seeded and sliced
1 tablespoon Thai fish sauce
2 tablespoons lime juice
2 scallions, chopped, and
cilantro leaves, to garnish

SERVES 4–6

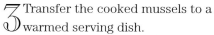

3 Transfer the cooked mussels to a warmed serving dish.

1 Place all the ingredients, except for the scallions and cilantro, in a large saucepan and stir thoroughly.

2 Cover and steam for 5–7 minutes, shaking the saucepan occasionally, until the mussels open. Discard any mussels that do not open.

4 Garnish the mussels with chopped scallions and cilantro leaves, and serve immediately.

FISH CAKES WITH CUCUMBER RELISH

These wonderful fish cakes are a familiar and popular appetizer, usually accompanied by Thai beer.

INGREDIENTS
12 ounces white fish fillet, such as cod,
cut into chunks
2 tablespoons red curry paste
1 egg
2 tablespoons Thai fish sauce
1 teaspoon sugar
2 tablespoons cornstarch
3 kaffir lime leaves, shredded
1 tablespoon chopped cilantro
2 ounces green beans, finely sliced
oil, for frying
Chinese mustard greens, to garnish

FOR THE CUCUMBER RELISH
¼ cup Thai coconut
or rice vinegar
¼ cup water
¼ cup sugar
1 head of pickled garlic
1 cucumber, quartered and sliced
4 shallots, finely sliced
1 tablespoon finely chopped ginger
2 red chilies, seeded and finely sliced

MAKES ABOUT 12

1 To make the cucumber relish, bring the vinegar, water and sugar to a boil. Stir until the sugar dissolves, then remove from the heat and cool.

2 Combine the rest of the ingredients for the relish in a bowl and pour them into the vinegar mixture.

3 Combine the fish, curry paste and egg in a food processor and process well. Transfer the mixture to a bowl, add the rest of the ingredients, except for the oil and garnish, and mix well.

4 Mold and shape the mixture into cakes. Make these about 2 inches in diameter and ¼ inch in thickness.

5 Heat the oil in a wok or deep-fat fryer. Fry the fish cakes, a few at a time, for 4–5 minutes or until golden brown. Remove and drain on paper towels. Garnish with Chinese mustard greens and serve with the cucumber relish.

CHIANG MAI NOODLE SOUP

A signature dish of the city of Chiang Mai, this delicious noodle soup has Burmese origins and is the Thai equivalent of the Malaysian Laksa.

INGREDIENTS
2½ cups coconut milk
2 tablespoons red curry paste
1 teaspoon ground turmeric
1 pound chicken thighs, boned and cut into bite-size chunks
2½ cups chicken stock
¼ cup Thai fish sauce
1 tablespoon dark soy sauce
juice of ½–1 lime
1 pound fresh egg noodles, blanched briefly in boiling water
salt and freshly ground black pepper

FOR THE GARNISH
3 scallions, chopped
4 red chilies, seeded and chopped
4 shallots, chopped
¼ cup sliced pickled mustard leaves, rinsed
2 tablespoons fried sliced garlic
cilantro leaves
4 fried noodle nests (optional)

SERVES 4–6

1 Put one third of the coconut milk into a large saucepan, bring to a boil and stir with a wooden spoon until it separates.

2 Add the curry paste and ground turmeric, stir to mix completely and cook until fragrant.

3 Add the chicken and stir-fry for about 2 minutes, ensuring that all the chunks are coated with the paste.

4 Add the remaining coconut milk, chicken stock, fish sauce and soy sauce. Season with salt and freshly ground black pepper to taste. Simmer gently for 7–10 minutes. Remove from the heat and stir in the lime juice.

5 Reheat the noodles in boiling water, drain and divide into individual bowls. Divide the chicken between the bowls and ladle in the hot soup. Top each serving with a few of each of the garnishes.

HOT AND SOUR SHRIMP SOUP WITH LEMONGRASS

This is a classic seafood soup – *Tom Yam Goong* – and is probably the most popular of Thai soups.

INGREDIENTS

1 pound jumbo shrimp (raw or cooked)
4 cups chicken stock or water
3 lemongrass stalks
10 kaffir lime leaves, torn in half
1 can (8 ounces) straw mushrooms, drained
3 tablespoons Thai fish sauce
¼ cup lime juice
2 tablespoons chopped scallions
1 tablespoon cilantro leaves
4 red chilies, seeded and chopped

SERVES 4–6

1 Shell and devein the shrimp and set aside. Rinse the shrimp shells, place in a large saucepan with the stock and bring to a boil.

2 Bruise the lemongrass stalks with the blunt edge of a large knife and add them to the stock with half of the lime leaves. Simmer gently for 5–6 minutes, until the stalks change color and the stock is fragrant.

3 Strain the stock, return to the saucepan and reheat. Add the mushrooms and shrimp, then cook for a few minutes, or until the shrimp turn pink if raw.

4 Stir in the fish sauce, lime juice, scallions, cilantro, chilies and the rest of the lime leaves. Taste; adjust the flavor. It should be sour, salty, spicy and hot.

SPINACH AND BEAN CURD SOUP

An extremely delicate and mild-flavored soup that can be used to balance the heat from a hot Thai curry.

INGREDIENTS

2 tablespoons dried shrimp
4 cups chicken stock
8 ounces fresh bean curd, drained and cut into ¾-inch cubes
2 tablespoons Thai fish sauce
12 ounces fresh spinach leaves, thoroughly washed
freshly ground black pepper
2 scallions, finely sliced, to garnish

SERVES 4–6

1 Rinse and drain the dried shrimp. Combine the shrimp with the chicken stock in a saucepan and bring to a boil.

2 Add the bean curd and simmer for about 5 minutes. Season with fish sauce and black pepper to taste.

3 Tear the spinach leaves into bite-size pieces and add to the soup. Cook for another 1–2 minutes.

4 Remove the soup from the heat, ladle into bowls and sprinkle the finely sliced scallions on top, to garnish.

PUMPKIN AND COCONUT SOUP

Enriched with smooth coconut cream, this soup thrills the taste buds with a combination of exotic and delicious flavors.

INGREDIENTS
2 garlic cloves, crushed
4 shallots, finely chopped
½ teaspoon shrimp paste
1 tablespoon dried shrimp, soaked for 10 minutes and drained
1 lemongrass stalk, chopped
2 green chilies, seeded
2½ cups chicken stock
1 pound pumpkin, cut into ¾-inch-thick chunks
2½ cups coconut milk
2 tablespoons Thai fish sauce
1 teaspoon sugar
4 ounces small cooked shelled shrimp
salt and freshly ground black pepper
2 red chilies, seeded and finely sliced, and 10–12 basil leaves, to garnish

SERVES 4–6

1 Grind the garlic, shallots, shrimp paste, dried shrimp, lemongrass, green chilies and salt to taste into a paste.

2 In a large saucepan, bring the chicken stock to a boil, add the ground paste and stir to dissolve.

COOK'S TIP
Shrimp paste, which is made from ground shrimps fermented in brine, is used to give food a savory flavor.

3 Add the pumpkin chunks and simmer gently for 10–15 minutes or until the pumpkin is tender.

4 Stir in the coconut milk, then return to a simmer. Add the fish sauce, sugar and ground black pepper to taste.

5 Add the shrimp and cook until they are heated through. Serve garnished with the sliced red chilies and basil leaves.

MIXED VEGETABLES IN COCONUT MILK

 most delicious way of cooking vegetables. If you don't like highly spiced food, use fewer red chilies.

INGREDIENTS
1 pound mixed vegetables, such as eggplant, baby corn, carrots, green beans and patty pan squash
8 red chilies, seeded
2 lemongrass stalks, chopped
4 kaffir lime leaves, torn
2 tablespoons vegetable oil
1 cup coconut milk
2 tablespoons Thai fish sauce
salt
15–20 Thai or holy basil leaves (bai grapao), to garnish

SERVES 4–6

1 Cut the vegetables into uniform small chunks using a sharp knife.

2 Put the red chilies, lemongrass and kaffir lime leaves in a mortar and grind together with a pestle.

3 Heat the oil in a wok or large deep-frying pan. Add the chili mixture and fry for 2–3 minutes.

4 Stir in the coconut milk and bring to a boil. Add the vegetables and cook for about 5 minutes or until they are tender. Season with the fish sauce and salt, and garnish with Thai or holy basil leaves.

BAMBOO SHOOT SALAD

This salad, which has a hot and sharp flavor, originated in north-east Thailand. Use fresh, young bamboo shoots when you can find them, otherwise substitute canned bamboo shoots.

INGREDIENTS
1 can (14 ounces) whole bamboo shoots
2 tablespoons glutinous rice
2 tablespoons chopped shallots
1 tablespoon chopped garlic
3 tablespoons chopped scallions
2 tablespoons Thai fish sauce
2 tablespoons lime juice
1 teaspoon sugar
½ teaspoon dried flaked chilies
20–25 small mint leaves
1 tablespoon toasted sesame seeds

SERVES 4

1 Rinse and drain the bamboo shoots, finely slice and set aside.

2 Dry-roast the rice in a frying pan until it is golden brown. Remove and grind to fine crumbs with a mortar and pestle.

3 Transfer the rice to a bowl, add the shallots, garlic, scallions, fish sauce, lime juice, sugar, chilies and half the mint leaves.

4 Mix thoroughly, then add to the bamboo shoots and toss. Serve sprinkled with sesame seeds and the remaining mint leaves.

LARP OF CHIANG MAI

Chiang Mai is a city in the northeast of Thailand. The city is culturally very close to Laos and famous for its chicken salad, which was originally called laap or larp. Duck, beef or pork can be used instead of chicken.

INGREDIENTS
1 pound ground chicken
1 lemongrass stalk, finely chopped
3 kaffir lime leaves, finely chopped
4 red chilies, seeded and chopped
¼ cup lime juice
2 tablespoons Thai fish sauce
1 tablespoon ground roasted rice
2 scallions, chopped
2 tablespoons cilantro leaves
mixed lettuce leaves, to serve
cucumber and tomato slices, and a few
sprigs of mint, to garnish

SERVES 4–6

1 Heat a large non-stick frying pan. Add the ground chicken, and a little water to moisten while cooking.

2 Stir constantly until cooked; this will take 7–10 minutes.

3 Transfer the cooked chicken to a large bowl and add the rest of the ingredients. Mix thoroughly.

4 Serve on a bed of mixed lettuce leaves and garnish with cucumber and tomato slices and a few sprigs of mint.

COOK'S TIP
Use sticky, or glutinous, rice to make ground roasted rice. Put the rice in a frying pan and dry-roast until golden brown. Remove and grind to a powder in a mortar and pestle or in a food processor. Keep in a glass jar in a cool and dry place and use as needed.

CABBAGE SALAD

A simple and delicious way of using cabbage. Other vegetables such as broccoli, cauliflower and Chinese cabbage can also be used.

INGREDIENTS
2 tablespoons Thai fish sauce
grated rind of 1 lime
2 tablespoons lime juice
½ cup coconut milk
2 tablespoons vegetable oil
2 large red chilies, seeded and
cut into fine strips
6 garlic cloves, finely sliced
6 shallots, finely sliced
1 small cabbage, shredded
2 tablespoons coarsely chopped roasted
peanuts, to serve

SERVES 4–6

1 Make the dressing by combining the fish sauce, lime rind and juice and coconut milk. Set aside.

2 Heat the oil in a wok or frying pan. Stir-fry the chilies, garlic and shallots until the shallots are brown and crisp. Remove from the heat and set aside.

3 Blanch the cabbage in boiling salted water for 2–3 minutes, drain and put into a bowl.

4 Stir the dressing into the cabbage, toss and mix well. Transfer the salad to a serving dish. Sprinkle with the fried shallot mixture and the chopped roasted peanuts.

THAI BEEF SALAD

A hearty salad of beef, laced with a chili and lime dressing that perfectly complements the meat.

INGREDIENTS
4 sirloin steaks (8 ounces each)
1 red onion, finely sliced
½ cucumber, cut into thin ribbons
1 lemongrass stalk, finely chopped
2 tablespoons chopped scallions
juice of 2 limes
1–2 tablespoons Thai fish sauce
2–4 red chilies, thinly sliced, fresh cilantro, Chinese mustard greens and mint leaves, to garnish

SERVES 4

1 Pan-fry, broil or grill the steaks to medium-rare. Set aside to rest for 10–15 minutes.

2 When it is cool, thinly slice the beef and put the slices in a large bowl.

3 Add the sliced onion, cucumber ribbons and lemongrass.

4 Add the scallions. Toss and season with lime juice and fish sauce. Serve at room temperature or chilled, garnished with the sliced chilies, cilantro, Chinese mustard greens and mint leaves.

TANGY CHICKEN SALAD

his fresh and lively dish typifies the character of Thai cuisine. It is ideal for an appetizer or light lunch.

INGREDIENTS

4 skinned, boneless chicken breasts
2 garlic cloves, crushed and
roughly chopped
2 tablespoons soy sauce
2 tablespoons vegetable oil
½ cup coconut milk
2 tablespoons Thai fish sauce
juice of 1 lime
2 tablespoons palm or light brown sugar
½ cup water chestnuts, sliced
¼ cup cashews, roasted
4 shallots, finely sliced
4 kaffir lime leaves, finely sliced
1 lemongrass stalk, finely sliced
1 teaspoon chopped galangal
1 large red chili, seeded and
finely sliced
2 scallions, finely sliced
10–12 mint leaves, torn
1 head lettuce, to serve
sprigs of cilantro and 2 red chilies,
seeded and sliced, to garnish

SERVES 4–6

1 Trim the chicken breasts of any excess fat and put them in a large dish. Rub with the garlic, soy sauce and 1 tablespoon of the oil. Let marinate for 1–2 hours.

2 Grill or pan-fry the chicken for 3–4 minutes on both sides or until cooked. Remove and set aside to cool.

3 In a small saucepan, heat the coconut milk, fish sauce, lime juice and palm sugar. Stir until all the sugar has dissolved and then remove from the heat.

4 Cut the cooked chicken into strips and combine with the water chestnuts, cashews, shallots, kaffir lime leaves, lemongrass, galangal, red chili, scallions and mint leaves.

5 Pour the coconut dressing over the chicken, toss and mix well. Serve the chicken on a bed of lettuce leaves and garnish with sprigs of cilantro and sliced red chilies.

BAKED FISH IN BANANA LEAVES

F ish that is prepared in this way is particularly succulent and flavorful. Fillets are used here rather than whole fish because they're easier for those who don't like to deal with bones. It is a great dish for outdoor barbecues.

INGREDIENTS
1 cup coconut milk
2 tablespoons red curry paste
3 tablespoons Thai fish sauce
2 tablespoons superfine sugar
5 kaffir lime leaves, torn
4 fish fillets (6 ounces each),
such as snapper
1 cup finely shredded mixed vegetables,
such as carrots and leeks
4 banana leaves
2 tablespoons shredded scallions,
and 2 red chilies, finely sliced,
to garnish

SERVES 4

1 Combine the coconut milk, curry paste, fish sauce, sugar and kaffir lime leaves in a shallow dish.

2 Marinate the fish in this mixture for 15–30 minutes. Preheat the oven to 400°F.

3 Combine the vegetables and lay a portion on top of a banana leaf. Place a piece of fish on top, together with a little of its marinade.

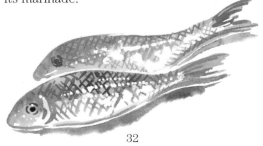

4 Wrap the fish up by turning in the sides and ends of the leaf. Secure with toothpicks. Repeat with the rest of the leaves and fish.

5 Bake for 20–25 minutes or until the fish is cooked. Alternatively, cook under the broiler or on the barbecue. Just before serving, garnish with a sprinkling of scallions and sliced red chilies.

STIR-FRIED SCALLOPS WITH ASPARAGUS

Asparagus is extremely popular among the Thais. The combination of garlic and black pepper gives this dish its spiciness. You can substitute shrimp or other firm fish for the scallops, if desired.

INGREDIENTS
¼ cup vegetable oil
1 bunch asparagus, cut into
2-inch lengths
4 garlic cloves, finely chopped
2 shallots, finely chopped
1 pound scallops, cleaned
2 tablespoons Thai fish sauce
½ teaspoon coarsely ground
black pepper
½ cup coconut milk
cilantro leaves, to garnish

SERVES 4–6

1 Heat half the oil in a wok or large frying pan. Add the asparagus and stir-fry for about 2 minutes. Transfer the asparagus to a plate and set aside.

2 Add the rest of the oil, garlic and shallots to the same wok and fry until fragrant. Add the scallops, stir and cook for another 1–2 minutes.

3 Return the asparagus to the wok. Add the fish sauce, ground black pepper and coconut milk.

4 Stir and cook for another 3–4 minutes or until the scallops and asparagus are cooked. Garnish with the cilantro leaves.

SATAY SHRIMP

n enticing and tasty dish. Lightly cooked greens and jasmine rice make good accompaniments.

INGREDIENTS

1 pound jumbo shrimp, shelled and deveined, tails intact
½ bunch cilantro leaves, 4 red chilies, finely sliced, and scallions, cut diagonally, to garnish

FOR THE PEANUT SAUCE

3 tablespoons vegetable oil
1 tablespoon chopped garlic
1 small onion, chopped
3–4 red chilies, crushed and chopped
3 kaffir lime leaves, torn
1 lemongrass stalk, bruised and chopped
1 teaspoon medium curry paste
1 cup coconut milk
1-inch cinnamon stick
½ cup crunchy peanut butter
3 tablespoons tamarind juice
2 tablespoons Thai fish sauce
2 tablespoons palm or light brown sugar juice of ½ lemon

SERVES 4–6

1 To make the sauce, heat half the oil in a wok or large frying pan and add the garlic and onion. Cook until they soften, 3–4 minutes.

2 Add the chilies, kaffir lime leaves, lemongrass and curry paste. Cook for another 2–3 minutes.

3 Stir in the coconut milk, cinnamon stick, peanut butter, tamarind juice, fish sauce, palm sugar and lemon juice.

4 Reduce the heat and simmer gently for 15–20 minutes or until the sauce thickens, stirring occasionally so that the sauce doesn't stick to the bottom of the wok or frying pan.

5 Heat the rest of the oil in a wok or large frying pan. Add the shrimp and stir-fry for 3–4 minutes or until the shrimp turn pink and are slightly firm to the touch.

6 Mix the shrimp with the sauce. Serve garnished with cilantro leaves, red chilies and scallions.

SWEET AND SOUR PORK, THAI-STYLE

S weet-and-sour is traditionally a Chinese creation, but the Thais also do it very well. This version has a fresh and clean flavor and makes a good one-dish meal when served over rice.

INGREDIENTS
12 ounces pork tenderloin
2 tablespoons vegetable oil
4 garlic cloves, finely sliced
1 small red onion, sliced
2 tablespoons Thai fish sauce
1 tablespoon sugar
1 red bell pepper, seeded and diced
½ cucumber, seeded and sliced
2 plum tomatoes, cut into wedges
4 ounces pineapple, cut into small chunks
2 scallions, cut into short lengths
freshly ground black pepper
cilantro leaves and scallions, shredded, to garnish

SERVES 4

1 Slice the pork into thin strips. Heat the oil in a wok or large frying pan.

2 Add the garlic and fry until golden, then add the pork and stir-fry for 4–5 minutes. Add the onion.

3 Season with fish sauce, sugar and freshly ground black pepper. Stir and cook for 3–4 minutes or until the pork is fully cooked.

4 Add the rest of the vegetables, the pineapple and scallions. You may need to add a few tablespoons of water. Continue to stir-fry for another 3–4 minutes. Serve hot, garnished with cilantro leaves and scallions.

BARBECUED CHICKEN

Barbecued chicken is served almost everywhere in Thailand, from portable sidewalk stands to sports stadiums and beaches. For an authentic touch, serve with rice on a banana leaf.

INGREDIENTS
1 chicken (3–3½ pounds),
cut into 8–10 pieces
2 limes, cut into wedges,
2 red chilies, finely sliced, and
a few lemongrass stalks, to garnish

FOR THE MARINADE
2 lemongrass stalks, chopped
1-inch piece fresh ginger
6 garlic cloves
4 shallots
½ bunch cilantro roots
1 tablespoon palm or light brown sugar
½ cup coconut milk
2 tablespoons Thai fish sauce
2 tablespoons soy sauce

SERVES 4–6

1 To make the marinade, put all the ingredients into a food processor and process until smooth.

2 Put the chicken pieces in a dish and pour the marinade over them. Leave in a cool place to marinate for at least 4 hours or preferably overnight.

3 Barbecue the chicken over glowing coals, or place it on a rack set over a baking tray and bake at 400°F for 20–30 minutes or until the chicken is cooked and golden brown. Turn the pieces occasionally and brush with the marinade.

4 Garnish with lime wedges, finely sliced red chilies and lemongrass.

IR-FRIED CHICKEN WITH BASIL AND CHILIES

This quick and easy chicken dish is an excellent introduction to Thai cuisine. Deep frying the basil adds another dimension to this recipe. Thai basil, also known as holy basil, has a unique, pungent flavor that is both spicy and sharp. The dull leaves have serrated edges.

INGREDIENTS
3 tablespoons vegetable oil
4 garlic cloves, sliced
2–4 red chilies, seeded and chopped
1 chicken (1 pound), cut into
bite-size pieces
2–3 tablespoons Thai fish sauce
2 teaspoons dark soy sauce
1 teaspoon sugar
10–12 Thai basil leaves
2 red chilies, finely sliced, and
20 Thai basil leaves, deep fried
(optional), to garnish

SERVES 4–6

COOK'S TIP
To deep fry Thai basil leaves, make sure that the leaves are completely dry. Deep fry in hot oil for 30–40 seconds, lift out and drain on paper towels.

1 Heat the oil in a wok or large frying pan and swirl it around.

2 Add the garlic and chilies and stir-fry until golden.

3 Add the chicken and stir-fry until it changes color.

4 Season with fish sauce, soy sauce and sugar. Continue to stir-fry for another 3–4 minutes or until the chicken is cooked through. Stir in the fresh Thai basil leaves. Garnish with sliced red chilies and the deep fried basil, if using.

FRAGRANT THAI MEATBALLS

 creamy peanut sauce accompanies these tasty little meatballs, which can be made from pork or beef.

INGREDIENTS
1 pound lean ground pork or beef
1 tablespoon chopped garlic
1 lemongrass stalk, finely chopped
4 scallions, finely chopped
1 tablespoon chopped fresh cilantro
2 tablespoons red curry paste
1 tablespoon lemon juice
1 tablespoon Thai fish sauce
1 egg
salt and freshly ground black pepper
rice flour, for dusting
oil, for deep frying
sprigs of cilantro, to garnish

FOR THE PEANUT SAUCE
1 tablespoon vegetable oil
1 tablespoon red curry paste
2 tablespoons crunchy peanut butter
1 tablespoon palm or light brown sugar
1 tablespoon lemon juice
1 cup coconut milk

SERVES 4–6

1 Make the peanut sauce. Heat the oil in a small saucepan, add the curry paste and fry for 1 minute.

2 Stir in the rest of the ingredients for the sauce, and bring to a boil. Lower the heat and simmer for about 5 minutes, or until the sauce thickens.

3 Make the meatballs. Combine all the ingredients except for the rice flour, oil and cilantro, and add some seasoning. Combine everything well.

4 Roll and shape the meat into small balls about the size of a walnut. Dust the meatballs with rice flour.

5 Heat the oil in a wok until hot, and deep fry the meatballs in batches until nicely browned and cooked through. Drain on paper towels. Serve garnished with sprigs of cilantro and accompanied by the peanut sauce.

STIR-FRIED BEEF IN OYSTER SAUCE

Another simple but delicious recipe. In Thailand, fresh straw mushrooms are readily available, but oyster mushrooms make a good substitute. To make the dish even more interesting, use several types of mushroom.

INGREDIENTS

1 pound rump steak
2 tablespoons soy sauce
1 tablespoon cornstarch
3 tablespoons vegetable oil
1 tablespoon chopped garlic
1 tablespoon chopped ginger
8 ounces mixed mushrooms, such as shiitake, oyster and straw
2 tablespoons oyster sauce
1 teaspoon sugar
4 scallions, cut into short lengths
freshly ground black pepper
2 red chilies, cut into strips, to garnish

SERVES 4–6

COOK'S TIP
Made from extracts of oysters, oyster sauce is velvety smooth and has a savory-sweet and meaty taste. There are several types available; buy the best you can afford.

1 Slice the beef, on the diagonal, into long thin strips. Combine the soy sauce and cornstarch in a large bowl, stir in the beef and let marinate for 1–2 hours.

2 Heat half the oil in a wok or frying pan. Add the garlic and ginger and fry until fragrant. Stir in the strips of beef. Stir to separate the pieces, let them color and cook for 1–2 minutes. Remove from the pan and set aside.

3 Heat the remaining oil in the wok. Add your selection of mixed mushrooms and cook until tender.

4 Return the beef to the wok with the mushrooms. Add the oyster sauce, sugar and freshly ground black pepper to taste. Mix well.

5 Add the scallions. Stir well. Serve garnished with strips of red chili.

MUSSAMAN CURRY

This curry is Indian in origin. Traditionally it is made with beef, but chicken or lamb can be used, or you can make a vegetarian version using bean curd. It has a rich, sweet and spicy flavor. Serve with boiled rice.

INGREDIENTS

2½ cups coconut milk
1½ pounds stewing beef, cut into
1-inch chunks
1 cup coconut cream
3 tablespoons Mussaman curry paste
(see Cook's Tip)
2 tablespoons Thai fish sauce
1 tablespoon palm or light brown sugar
¼ cup tamarind juice
6 cardamom pods
1 cinnamon stick
8 ounces potatoes, cut into
uniform chunks
1 onion, cut into wedges
¼ cup roasted peanuts
boiled rice, to serve

SERVES 4–6

1 Bring the coconut milk to a gentle boil in a large saucepan. Add the beef and simmer until tender – about 40 minutes.

2 Put the coconut cream in a saucepan, then cook for 5–8 minutes, stirring constantly, until it separates.

3 Add the Mussaman curry paste and fry until fragrant. Add the fried curry paste to the pan containing the cooked beef.

4 Add the fish sauce, sugar, tamarind juice, cardamom pods, cinnamon stick, potato chunks and onion. Simmer for 10-15 minutes, or until the potatoes are cooked.

5 Add the roasted peanuts. Cook for another 5 minutes, then serve with rice.

COOK'S TIP

Mussaman curry paste is used to make the Thai version of a Muslim curry. It can be prepared and then stored in a glass jar in the fridge for up to four months.
Remove the seeds from 12 large dried chilies and soak the chilies in hot water for 15 minutes. Combine 4 tablespoons chopped shallots, 5 garlic cloves, 1 chopped lemongrass stalk, 2 teaspoons chopped galangal, 1 teaspoon cumin seeds, 1 tablespoon coriander seeds, 2 cloves and 6 black peppercorns. Place in a wok and dry-fry over low heat for 5–6 minutes. Grind or process into a powder and stir in 1 teaspoon shrimp paste, 1 teaspoon salt, 1 teaspoon sugar and 2 tablespoons oil.

CURRIED SHRIMP IN COCONUT MILK

 currylike dish in which shrimp are cooked in a wonderful, spicy coconut gravy.

INGREDIENTS
2½ cups coconut milk
2 tablespoons yellow curry paste
(see Cook's Tip)
1 tablespoon Thai fish sauce
½ teaspoon salt
1 teaspoon sugar
1 pound jumbo shrimp, shelled and
deveined, tails intact
8 ounces cherry tomatoes
juice of ½ lime, to serve
2 red chilies, cut into strips, and cilantro
leaves, to garnish

SERVES 4–6

1 Put half the coconut milk into a pan or wok and bring to a boil.

2 Add the yellow curry paste to the coconut milk, stir until it disperses, then simmer for about 10 minutes.

3 Add the fish sauce, salt, sugar and remaining coconut milk. Simmer for another 5 minutes.

4 Add the shrimp and cherry tomatoes. Simmer gently for about 5 minutes until the shrimp are pink and tender.

5 Serve sprinkled with lime juice and garnished with chilies and cilantro.

COOK'S TIP
To make yellow curry paste, process together 6–8 yellow chilies, 1 chopped lemongrass stalk, 4 peeled shallots, 4 garlic cloves, 1 tablespoon peeled chopped ginger, 1 teaspoon coriander seeds, 1 teaspoon mustard powder, 1 teaspoon salt, ½ teaspoon ground cinnamon, 1 tablespoon light brown sugar and 2 tablespoons oil in a food processor. When a paste has formed, transfer it to a jar and chill.

Bean Curd and Green Bean Red Curry

This is another curry that is simple and quick to make. This recipe uses green beans, but you can use almost any kind of vegetable, such as eggplant, bamboo shoots or broccoli.

Ingredients
2½ cups coconut milk
1 tablespoon red curry paste
3 tablespoons Thai fish sauce
2 teaspoons palm or light brown sugar
8 ounces button mushrooms
4 ounces green beans, trimmed
6 ounces bean curd, rinsed and cut into
¾-inch cubes
4 kaffir lime leaves, torn
2 red chilies, sliced
cilantro leaves, to garnish

Serves 4–6

1 Put about one-third of the coconut milk in a wok or saucepan. Cook until it starts to separate and an oily sheen appears.

2 Add the red curry paste, fish sauce and sugar to the coconut milk. Stir well.

3 Add the mushrooms to the curry sauce. Stir and cook for 1 minute.

4 Stir in the rest of the coconut milk and bring back to a boil.

5 Add the green beans and bean curd and simmer gently for another 4–5 minutes.

6 Stir in the torn kaffir lime leaves and sliced chilies. Serve garnished with the cilantro leaves.

GREEN BEEF CURRY WITH THAI EGGPLANT

his is a very quick curry to make, so be sure to use tender, good-quality meat.

INGREDIENTS
3 tablespoons vegetable oil
2½ cups coconut milk
1 pound beef sirloin
4 kaffir lime leaves, torn
1–2 tablespoons Thai fish sauce
1 teaspoon palm or light brown sugar
5 ounces small Thai eggplant, halved
a small handful of Thai basil
2 green chilies, shredded to garnish

FOR THE GREEN CURRY PASTE
15 hot green chilies
2 lemongrass stalks, chopped
3 shallots, sliced
2 garlic cloves
1 tablespoon chopped galangal
4 kaffir lime leaves, chopped
½ teaspoon grated kaffir lime rind
1 teaspoon chopped cilantro root
6 black peppercorns
1 teaspoon coriander seeds, roasted
1 teaspoon cumin seeds, roasted
1 tablespoon sugar
1 teaspoon salt
1 teaspoon shrimp paste (optional)

SERVES 4–6

1 Make the green curry paste. Combine all the ingredients thoroughly. Pound them in a mortar and pestle or process in a food processor until smooth. Add 2 tablespoons of the oil, a little at a time, and blend well between each addition. Keep in a glass jar in the fridge until required.

2 Heat the remaining oil in a large saucepan or wok. Add 3 tablespoons green curry paste and fry until fragrant.

3 Stir in half the coconut milk, a little at a time. Cook for 5–6 minutes, until an oily sheen appears on the surface.

4 Cut the beef into long, thin slices and add to the saucepan with the kaffir lime leaves, fish sauce, sugar and eggplant. Cook for 2–3 minutes, then stir in the remaining coconut milk.

5 Bring back to a simmer and cook until the meat and eggplant are tender. Stir in the Thai basil just before serving. Garnish with the shredded green chilies.

FRIED JASMINE RICE

Thai basil, also known as holy basil, has a unique, pungent flavor that is both spicy and sharp. It can be found in most Asian food markets.

INGREDIENTS

3 tablespoons vegetable oil

1 egg, beaten

1 onion, chopped

1 tablespoon chopped garlic

1 tablespoon shrimp paste

4 cups cooked jasmine rice

12 ounces cooked shelled shrimp

¼ cup thawed frozen peas

oyster sauce, to taste

2 scallions, chopped

15–20 Thai basil leaves, roughly snipped, plus an extra sprig, to garnish

SERVES 4–6

1 Heat 1 tablespoon of the oil in a wok or frying pan. Add the beaten egg and swirl it around the pan to set like a thin pancake.

2 Cook the egg pancake until golden, slide it out onto a flat surface, roll it up and cut it into thin strips. Set aside.

3 Heat the remaining oil in the wok or large frying pan, add the onion and garlic and fry for 2–3 minutes. Stir in the shrimp paste and mix well.

4 Add the rice, shrimp and peas and toss together, until everything is heated through.

5 Season with oyster sauce to taste, taking great care as the shrimp paste is salty. Add the scallions and basil leaves. Serve topped with the strips of egg pancake. Garnish with a sprig of basil.

FRIED RICE WITH PORK

f desired, garnish this with strips of omelette, as in the recipe for Fried Jasmine Rice.

INGREDIENTS
3 tablespoons vegetable oil
1 onion, chopped
1 tablespoon chopped garlic
4 ounces pork tenderloin, cut into small cubes
2 eggs, beaten
4 cups cooked rice
2 tablespoons Thai fish sauce
1 tablespoon dark soy sauce
½ teaspoon superfine sugar
4 scallions, finely sliced, 2 red chilies, sliced, 1 lime, cut into wedges, and strips of omelette (optional), to garnish

SERVES 4–6

1 Heat the oil in a wok or large frying pan. Add the onion and garlic and cook for about 2 minutes, or until softened.

2 Add the pork to the softened onion and garlic. Stir-fry until the pork changes color and is thoroughly cooked.

3 Add the eggs and cook until scrambled into small lumps.

4 Add the rice and continue to stir and toss, in order to coat it with the oil and prevent it from sticking.

5 Add the fish sauce, soy sauce and sugar, and mix well. Continue to fry until the rice is thoroughly heated. Garnish with sliced scallions, red chilies and lime wedges.

SPECIAL CHOW MEIN

L ap cheong is a special air-dried Chinese sausage. It is available at most Chinese markets. If you cannot buy it, substitute diced ham, chorizo or salami.

INGREDIENTS

3 tablespoons vegetable oil
2 garlic cloves, sliced
1 teaspoon chopped ginger
2 red chilies, chopped
2 lap cheong (3 ounces each), rinsed
and sliced (optional)
1 boneless chicken breast, thinly sliced
16 uncooked tiger shrimp, shelled
and deveined, tails intact
4 ounces green beans
8 ounces bean sprouts
2 ounces garlic chives
1 pound egg noodles, cooked in boiling
water until tender
2 tablespoons soy sauce
1 tablespoon oyster sauce
1 tablespoon sesame oil
salt and freshly ground black pepper
2 scallions, shredded, and
1 tablespoon cilantro leaves,
to garnish

SERVES 4–6

1 Heat 1 tablespoon of the oil in a wok or large frying pan and fry the garlic, ginger and chilies. Add the lap cheong (or its substitute), chicken, shrimp and beans. Stir-fry over high heat for about 2 minutes or until the chicken and shrimp are cooked. Transfer the mixture to a bowl and set aside.

2 Heat the rest of the oil in the same wok. Add the beansprouts and garlic chives. Stir-fry for 1–2 minutes.

3 Add the noodles and toss and stir to mix. Season with soy sauce, oyster sauce, salt and pepper.

4 Return the shrimp mixture to the wok. Reheat and mix well with the noodles. Stir in the sesame oil. Serve garnished with scallions and cilantro leaves.

COCONUT RICE

T his dish is usually served with a tangy papaya salad to balance the richness of the coconut.

INGREDIENTS
2 cups jasmine rice
1 cup water
2 cups coconut milk
½ teaspoon salt
2 tablespoons sugar
fresh shredded coconut, to
garnish (optional)

SERVES 4–6

1 Wash the rice in several changes of cold water until the water runs clear. Put the water, coconut milk, salt and sugar in a heavy-based saucepan.

2 Add the rice, cover and bring to a boil. Reduce the heat to low and simmer for 15–20 minutes or until the rice is tender to the bite and cooked through.

3 Turn off the heat and allow the rice to rest in the pan for 5–10 minutes.

4 Fluff the rice with chopsticks before serving. Garnish, if desired, with fresh shredded coconut.

PINEAPPLE FRIED RICE

W hen buying a pineapple, look for a sweet-smelling fruit with an even brownish-yellow skin. To test for ripeness, tap the base – a dull sound indicates that the fruit is ripe. The flesh should also give slightly when pressed.

INGREDIENTS
1 pineapple
2 tablespoons vegetable oil
1 small onion, finely chopped
2 green chilies,
seeded and chopped
8 ounces pork tenderloin,
cut into small dice
4 ounces cooked shelled shrimp
3–4 cups cold cooked rice
¼ cup roasted cashews
2 scallions, chopped
2 tablespoons Thai fish sauce
1 tablespoon soy sauce
2 red chilies and 1 green chili, sliced,
and 10–12 mint leaves, to garnish

SERVES 4–6

1 Cut the pineapple in half lengthwise and remove the flesh from both halves by cutting around inside the skin. Reserve the shells. You need 4 ounces of fruit, chopped finely (keep the rest for dessert).

COOK'S TIP
This dish is ideal to prepare for a "special-occasion" meal. Served in the pineapple shells, it is sure to be the highlight of the meal.

2 Heat the oil in a wok or large frying pan. Add the onion and chilies and fry for 3–5 minutes or until softened. Add the pork and cook until it is brown on all sides.

3 Stir in the shrimp and rice and toss well. Continue to stir-fry until the rice is thoroughly heated. Add the chopped pineapple, cashews and scallions. Season with fish sauce and soy sauce.

4 Spoon into the pineapple shells. Garnish with shredded mint leaves and red and green chilies.

THAI FRIED NOODLES

Pad Thai has a fascinating flavor and texture. It is made with rice noodles and is considered one of the national dishes of Thailand.

INGREDIENTS

12 ounces rice noodles
3 tablespoons vegetable oil
1 tablespoon chopped garlic
16 uncooked jumbo shrimp, shelled and deveined, tails intact
2 eggs, lightly beaten
1 tablespoon dried shrimp, rinsed
2 tablespoons pickled white radish
2 ounces fried bean curd, cut into small slivers
½ teaspoon dried chili flakes
4 ounces garlic chives, cut into 2-inch lengths
8 ounces bean sprouts
¼ cup roasted peanuts, coarsely ground
1 teaspoon granulated sugar
1 tablespoon dark soy sauce
2 tablespoons Thai fish sauce
2 tablespoons tamarind juice
2 tablespoons cilantro leaves and 1 kaffir lime cut in wedges, to garnish

SERVES 4–6

1 Soak the noodles in warm water for 20–30 minutes, then drain.

2 Heat 1 tablespoon of the oil in a wok or large frying pan. Add the garlic and fry until golden. Stir in the shrimp and cook for 1–2 minutes until pink, tossing occasionally. Remove and set aside.

3 Heat another 1 tablespoon of oil in the wok. Add the eggs and tilt the wok to spread them into a thin sheet. Stir to scramble and break the egg into small pieces. Remove from the wok and set aside with the shrimp.

4 Heat the rest of the oil in the same wok. Add the dried shrimp, pickled white radish, fried bean curd and dried chili flakes. Stir briefly. Add the soaked noodles and stir-fry for 5 minutes.

5 Add the garlic chives, half the bean-sprouts and half the ground peanuts. Season with the sugar, soy sauce, fish sauce and tamarind juice. Mix well and cook until the noodles are heated through.

6 Return the shrimp and egg mixture to the wok and mix with the noodles. Serve garnished with the rest of the beansprouts, peanuts, cilantro leaves and lime wedges.

TAPIOCA PUDDING

This pudding, made from large, pearl tapioca and coconut milk, and served warm, is much lighter than the Western-style version. You can adjust the sweetness to your taste. Serve with lychees or the smaller, similar-tasting logans – also known as dragon's eyes.

INGREDIENTS
½ cup tapioca
2 cups water
¾ cup sugar
pinch of salt
1 cup coconut milk
9 ounces prepared tropical fruits
finely shredded rind of 1 lime,
to decorate

SERVES 4

1 Soak the tapioca in warm water for 1 hour, until the grains swell. Drain.

2 Put the water in a saucepan and bring to a boil. Stir in the sugar and salt.

3 Add the tapioca and coconut milk and simmer for about 10 minutes.

4 Serve warm with tropical fruits, and decorate with strips of lime rind.

FRIED BANANAS

These delicious treats are a favorite among both children and adults. They are sold as snacks throughout the day and night at portable roadside stands and markets. Other fruits, such as pineapple and apple, work just as well.

INGREDIENTS
½ cup flour
½ teaspoon baking soda
pinch of salt
2 tablespoons sugar
1 egg
6 tablespoons water
2 tablespoons shredded coconut, or
1 tablespoon sesame seeds
4 firm bananas
oil, for deep frying
lychees and sprigs of mint, to decorate
2 tablespoons honey, to serve (optional)

SERVES 4

1 Sift the flour, baking soda and salt into a bowl. Stir in the sugar. Whisk in the egg and add enough water to make a quite thin batter.

2 Whisk in the shredded coconut or sesame seeds.

3 Peel the bananas. Carefully cut each one in half lengthwise, and then crosswise.

4 Heat the oil in a wok or deep-frying pan. Dip the bananas in the batter, then deep-fry in batches in the oil until golden.

5 Remove from the oil and drain on paper towels. Decorate with lychees and mint sprigs and serve immediately with honey, if using.

STEWED PUMPKIN IN COCONUT CREAM

Stewed fruit is a popular dessert in Thailand. Use the firm-textured Japanese kabocha pumpkin for this dish, if you can. Bananas and melons can also be prepared in this way, as can corn or pulses such as mung beans and black beans.

INGREDIENTS
1 small pumpkin, about 2 pounds
3 cups coconut milk
¾ cup sugar
pinch of salt
pumpkin seeds, toasted, and
mint sprigs, to decorate

SERVES 4–6

COOK'S TIP
Any pumpkin can be used for this dish, as long as it has a firm texture. Jamaican or New Zealand varieties both make good alternatives to kabocha pumpkin.

1 Wash the pumpkin skin and cut off most of it. Scoop out the seeds.

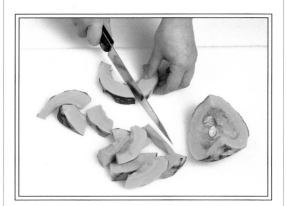

2 Using a sharp knife, cut the flesh into pieces about 2 inches long and ¾-inch wide.

3 In a saucepan, bring the coconut milk, sugar and salt to the boil.

4 Add the pumpkin and simmer for 10–15 minutes until the pumpkin is tender. Serve warm. Decorate each serving with a few toasted pumpkin seeds and a mint sprig.

BAKED RICE PUDDING, THAI-STYLE

Black glutinous rice, also known as black sticky rice, has long black grains and a nutty taste similar to wild rice. This baked pudding has a distinct character and flavor all of its own.

INGREDIENTS

¾ cup white or black glutinous (sticky) rice
2 tablespoons light brown sugar
2 cups coconut milk
1 cup water
3 eggs
2 tablespoons granulated sugar
confectioners' sugar, to decorate

SERVES 4–6

1 Combine the glutinous rice, brown sugar, half the coconut milk and all the water in a saucepan.

2 Bring to a boil and simmer for 15–20 minutes or until the rice has absorbed most of the liquid, stirring occasionally. Preheat the oven to 300°F.

3 Transfer the rice to one large ovenproof dish or divide it into individual ramekins. Combine the eggs, remaining coconut milk and sugar in a bowl.

4 Strain the mixture and pour evenly over the partially cooked rice.

5 Place the dish in a baking pan. Pour in enough boiling water to come halfway up the sides of the dish.

6 Cover the dish with a piece of tinfoil and bake for 35 minutes to 1 hour or until the custard is set. Serve warm or cold, sprinkled with confectioners' sugar.

MANGO WITH STICKY RICE

Everyone's favorite dessert. Mangoes, with their delicate fragrance, sweet-and-sour flavor and velvety flesh, blend especially well with coconut-flavored rice. You need to start preparing this dish the day before.

INGREDIENTS
½ cup white glutinous (sticky) rice
¾ cup thick coconut milk
3 tablespoons sugar
pinch of salt
2 ripe mangoes
strips of lime rind, to decorate

SERVES 4

1 Rinse the glutinous rice thoroughly in several changes of cold water, until the water is clear, then let soak overnight in a bowl of fresh, cold water.

2 Drain the rice and spread in an even layer in a steamer lined with some cheesecloth. Cover and steam for about 20 minutes, or until the grains of rice are tender and succulent.

3 Meanwhile, reserve 3 tablespoons of the top of the coconut milk and combine the rest with the sugar and salt in a saucepan. Bring to a boil, stirring until the sugar dissolves, then pour into a bowl and let cool a little.

4 Transfer the rice to a bowl and pour the coconut mixture over it. Stir, then leave for 10–15 minutes.

5 Peel the mangoes and cut the flesh into slices. Place the slices on top of the rice and drizzle the reserved coconut milk on top. Decorate with strips of lime rind.

COCONUT CUSTARD

This traditional dish can be baked or steamed and is often served with sweet glutinous rice and a selection of fruits such as mango and persimmon.

INGREDIENTS
4 eggs
½ cup light brown sugar
1 cup coconut milk
1 teaspoon vanilla, rose or jasmine extract
mint leaves and confectioners' sugar, to decorate

SERVES 4–6

COOK'S TIP
Coconut milk can be obtained directly from coconut flesh – this gives the creamiest milk. It is also available in a can, as a soluble powder and in block form. Coconut milk that is pre-packaged in this way makes a useful addition to sauces and dressings.

1 Preheat the oven to 300°F. Whisk the eggs and sugar in a bowl until smooth. Add the coconut milk and vanilla and blend well.

2 Strain the mixture and pour into individual ramekins or a cake pan.

3 Stand the ramekins or pan in a roasting pan. Carefully fill the pan with hot water to reach halfway up the outsides of the ramekins or tin.

4 Bake for 35–40 minutes or until the custards are set. Test with a fine skewer or toothpick.

5 Remove from the oven and let cool. Turn out of the ramekins and serve with sliced fruit. Decorate with mint leaves and confectioners' sugar.

INDEX